To Uncle Gordon

On your Birthday 2007.

Geoffrey, Debbie, Andrew & Diana.
x x x x.

AeroCyprus Publications

CYPRUS from the AIR

Published by
AeroCyprus Publications
Apartment 21
Skiathou Street 30
Mesa Geitonia
Limassol 4006
Cyprus

Copyright 2005 Denny Rowland
ISBN 9963-9132-0-2

Printed in China

A Denny Rowland Production

Captions
Front Cover
*Petra tou Romiou - the birthplace of
Aphrodite*

Inside Front Cover
Nicosia - the divided City

Inside Back Cover
Farming in the West

Back Cover
*Nicosia, Agia Napa Fishing Boats,
Stavrovouni Monastery and Tilliria*

Right
The clear waters of Fontana Amorosa

Page-2
The Municipal Open Air Theatre

View from the Cockpit - see text

Limassol Municipality
Open Air Theatre

The Art and Craft of Aerial Photography

My interest in flying light aircraft began in the early Seventies. It was the natural progression from my boyhood passion for building and flying model aircraft. I also had more than just a passing interest in photography and like many hobbies that run out of control and take over one's life, the various elements came together naturally and formed the basis of what has become a full time occupation. So, what is it like working in the air? Well it is just the same as working on the ground except for the pressure of some high level stressors. Noise, cold, turbulence, cramped conditions and split second time constraints, are just some of the elements that make up a quite hostile working environment. In reality, the job is probably quite different from most people's idealistic perception of gently floating about in the sky whilst picking off nice artistic views of perfectly arranged scenery. That never happens.

When one is working from fixed wing aircraft as opposed to helicopters, the time constraints are far more severe due to the high speeds. Most photographers would like a little time to spend on getting composition and exposure just right, the luxury of a tripod would also be nice but it is not a practical possibility in the air. Aerial Photography at the first attempt often turns out to be less than everyone's cup of tea. What one's eye sees in the camera viewfinder is not the same as what the inner ear balance mechanisms are sensing, this creates a scenario that forms a recipe for vertigo and acute motion sickness for the unaccustomed. When one is working with wide angle lenses, the aircraft must be banked and slewed around to stop parts of the aircraft being seen in the shot (see left insert). When working at low level this maneuvering can get quite violent.

I am often asked the question "do I fly and take pictures at the same time?" The honest answer is both yes and no. Professional aerial photography is without doubt a two man job. If you want the best results you must fly with the best. A pilot/photographer will fly the aircraft into the desired position and then hand over control to the overall pilot in command with the words "You Have" The honour of deciding where to shoot from, rests with the photographer alone. The special relationship required to work efficiently in the air needs to be, above all, based on a well practiced routine. The cockpit is no place to have misunderstandings of any kind. When I am flying the aircraft the other pilot is watching out for other aircraft and terrain clearance heights, he also negotiates with air traffic control to get clearances to enter controlled airspace, whilst monitoring the aircraft's systems. Time is money, so a sound working routine is paramount to the overall success of each flight. One's instincts and experience are constantly being put to the test. For this reason I must salute the many pilots that I have flown with over the years, for their professionalism and their great contribution to my work.

The risks associated with working from light aircraft are minimal in comparison to the job satisfaction that it can bring. It has a few disappointments and some very special moments, but I always like to keep in mind the reality of what I am doing. Over the years and in rare moments of human and mechanical failure, some pilots and photographers have gone down and sadly were lost, this book is dedicated to those people.

After moving to Cyprus in the latter part of 2004, I met Avgostinos Avgousti. He is the chief flying instructor at Griffon Aviation at Pafos International Airport. After explaining what it was that I was intending to do, I was expecting the usual verbal exchange of why you cannot do that in Cyprus. As the corners of his mouth betrayed a grin I knew I had found my man. It is our combined efforts that you see in this book. Avgostinos has an extensive knowledge of the Island and has navigated us to every nook and cranny from the lofty peaks of Mount Olympus to the low level sea caves of Agia Napa. There are many military flight restrictions that control one's movements in the Cyprus Airspace, and none of this would have been possible without the co-operation of the Department of Civil Aviation and the Cyprus National Guard, who must approve and certify all material before release into the public domain. I must also thank the Cyprus Tourism Office for their help.

PZL 104 Wilga 80 - the perfect aerial photography platform.
To date we have flown over two thousand sorties together.

For those with a technical interest in photography, the equipment used for capturing this imagery is the same as can be purchased at any good pro-sumer camera store. A Canon 1Ds Mk1 with a set of image stabilised lenses was used for the vast majority of the shots, with a Kodak Pro SLR/c used as a back-up camera. Further stabilisation was achieved by the use of Kenyon KS-8 Gyro stabilisers fitted underneath the camera bodies. Data was stored in-camera on two gigabyte CF cards and downloaded to a laptop after landing. A Garmin GPS unit was linked to the camera to encode each image with exact positioning data. A Pentax 6x7 medium format film camera was also used but the age of digital has arrived - and is here to stay. Having the right equipment and not too much of it, does make a difference to the overall quality of the work, but at the end of the day, it is only a tool for conveying one's artistry in the simple act of recording a moment in time as seen from above.

The true art of aerial photography is found in the relentless task of searching with ones eyes wide open, to find what is there.

Argaka, Gialia and Tilliria area

Introduction

At a crucial point between Europe, Asia and Africa, in the North Eastern corner of the Mediterranean, you will find the Island of Cyprus. Its long and tempestuous past reveals a constant struggle against invaders from many nations eager to control this strategically important part of the World. A beautiful Island blessed with a warm and pleasant climate, it is today one of the most popular holiday venues in the Mediterranean. It has been said many times before, that nowhere else on the Planet will you find such a varied and rich environment, both man-made and natural, within such a small area.

For the first time Cyprus can be seen from the air to reveal it's true splendour. It is not surprising that the wonderful Greek imagination chose Cyprus as the birthplace of Aphrodite, the goddess of love and beauty. It is said that "a picture is worth a thousand words," so this book does not attempt to repeat what has been written before. Instead it sets out to reveal, by way of a magic carpet ride in the sky, a flight commentary describing the most interesting, ecologically significant and historically relevant places, as seen from above. Also included, are some of the Island's many fine hotels, these have formed the backbone of the Cyprus commercial development in tourism.

Cyprus is administratively divided into six districts (Pafos, Limassol, Larnaka, Famagusta, Nicosia and Kyrenia). Kyrenia lies entirely within the occupied area in the North of the Island with parts of Famagusta and Larnaka also falling within the Turkish controlled area. **Cyprus from the Air** is laid out to

cover each district as a separate colour coded chapter .

The Pafos Flight Route

Our aerial exploration starts in the west and features the Pafos District. After take-off from Pafos International Airport, we head northwest and arrive just south of Pomos, and then head-off southwest along the Chrysochou coastal plain towards Cape Arnautis. The spectacular mosaics of colour along the foothills of the Tilliria mountain range, reveal centuries of hard labour that have formed a traditional tier system of arable farmland. Copper mining was once a major industry here, and the export jetty still remains in

place. Today. the whole area predominantly grows fruit and vegetables, with vineyards that extend high into the Troodos Mountains. The majesty of mountains never fails to impress and they have been an inspiration for human societies and culture since time immemorial. Millions of visitors will come to experience the scenery and relax in the peace and tranquillity, whilst others may prefer to ski on the snow trails of Mount Olympus during the winter months.

However, globally all is not well with the mountains. For centuries their remoteness has protected them from the excesses of human exploitation. Mountain environments cover a large portion of the Earth's land surface, and half of the World population depends on those resources. In Cyprus the importance of the mountains is clearly evident when one turns on a tap. Mountains are the water towers of the world and are vital to all life on earth. Over the Island's known history, man has learned to live in the mountains by creating terraces, that after two millenniums can still support viable agriculture. The sustainability of the local ecosystem is a fine balance and one that can only be influenced by the sole guardians who have lived there for generations.

The maritime significance of the Mediterranean Sea is rich in cultural and historical importance; positioned centrally along the Chrysochou Bay one finds the popular harbour and new marina of Latchi (Lakki). It has become an annual meeting place for sailors from all over the World. This picturesque fishing village is famous for its many fine fish restaurants. Polis, a small ancient village close by, offers almost unlimited stretches of sandy and pebbled beaches.

Beyond Latchi and Polis, the old village of Neo Chorio is to be found. It is situated in the hills of the Akamas Peninsular with traditional tavernas and breathtaking views. As we head towards Cape Akamas we find The Anassa, a seven star luxury hotel, often frequented by the rich and famous. The Anassa, or Queen in Modern Greek, was recently made famous by the business tycoon Philip Green who allegedly hired all 192 suites and spent over five million Cyprus pounds on his fiftieth birthday celebrations.

Approaching the most westerly point of Cyprus we can see the Baths of Aphrodite, (Loutra Aphoditis), where it is said swimming in the clear blue waters of Fontana Amorosa, may help regain your youth.

Pressing on towards Cape Akamas, the barely visible tiny Mazaki Islet passes below us. It is the most westerly point of Cyprus. The Akamas mountain range leads us onto a Southerly heading towards Lara Point, where one will find the protected area of the Sea Turtle hatchery. It was set up in 1987 at Lara Bay.

Many regard the Akamas Peninsula as the most unspoilt part of the Island. It is an area of outstanding natural beauty and also one of great bio-diversity and ecological significance. As we move towards the Akamas Gorge and Cape Drepano we find the tiny Geronisos Island.

Fontana Amorosa Sunset

We continue towards the Coral Bay area passing over Pegeia Basilica, (Kantarkastoi), where we find an amazing labyrinth of sea caves and rocks with an inviting deep blue sea. Swimmers should give some respect to this area; sudden high winds and dangerous currents have, in the past, claimed lives.

As we enter Coral Bay we find the main tourist area with many fine hotels. The view of a familiar place when seen from above, can sometimes have a quite disorienting effect leading to some interesting discussions. In fact an abundance of hotels line this section of coast almost continuously into Kato Pafos.

Pafos Castle can be found in the harbour bay area and is popular with tourists throughout the year. The Castle hosts open-air theatre productions and the whole area offers a wealth of shopping opportunities and restaurants.

As we pass overhead Pafos International Airport, we come to the extensive developments at Aphrodite Hills and the Secret Valley complexes. Both have excellent golf facilities and adjacent luxury homes. Aphrodite Hills boasts a championship course with the impressive Intercontinental Hotel as its centrepiece. The Secret Valley 18-hole course is situated in a natural valley and course watering comes from its own irrigation system. The area also reveals some spectacular rock formations.

The once tedious journey from Limassol to Pafos has recently been vastly improved with the superbly engineered A6 highway. Running to the north of the old coast road, it has some impressive bridges that span deep valleys. It carves its way around many hillsides and cuts its way through the Paramali tunnel.

We now fly north to investigate the central part of the Pafos district where enroute we find the Asprokremos Dam. The Dam's staggering beauty is equalled only by its functionality to collect precious water from the Xeros Potamos River.

Continuing northwest, we find some interesting landscape at Episkopi Village. Our present heading then takes us on to the Donald Steel designed Tsada golf course, which is located on an elevated position 550 meters above sea level, in the former grounds of the Stavros tis Minthis Monastery. This is another fine Par 72 -6060 metre 18-hole course, offering a high standard of golf to those who enjoy the challenge of a well matured, tree-lined course.

Between the Akamas Forest and the Pafos Forest one sees a vast area of terraced arable farmland. This traditional way of farming can only be appreciated as an almost abstract art form when viewed from above. The Evretou Dam and the Mavrokolypos Dam are also to be found in this area and are well stocked with seventeen species of fish. Anglers should remember that they are required to purchase a local licence for each Dam before fishing there.

Our aerial tour of the Pafos District is now complete and it is time to take up our position behind a landing Airbus A320 at Pafos Internatioanl Airport. Our next task is to prepare in readiness for our flight of discovery over the Limassol District.

Latchi (Lakki) Harbour

Pomos Point

Copper Mine - Tilliria

Fontana Amorosa - Cape Arnaoutis - Akamas Peninsula

The Baths of Aphrodite

Pirgos Tis Regenas (Tower of the Queen) at Fontana Amorosa

The Island's most westerly point - Mazaki Islet

Lara Point - The Bay is well known as a protected hatchery for the Green Sea and Loggerhead Turtle

Cape Arnaoutis - Fontana Amorosa

Nowhere in the World is there sailing quite like the Mediterranean. The historic and cultural significance of Cyprus brings sailors from all over the Globe to share their passion. Marinas such as Latchi have become an annual meeting place for many

Latchi (Lakki) Harbour and Marina

Cape Arnaoutis - Fontana Amorosa

The Pegeia Basilica: cracks in the strata of chalk rocks have led to sea erosion, thus creating a labyrinth of sea caves

The Akamas Peninsula is regarded by many as the most isolated and unspoilt area in Cyprus. It is an area of outstanding natural beauty and also one of great bio-diversity and ecological significance. It is a paradise for nature lovers and is said to have been named after the hero Akamas who returned to Cyprus after the Trojan War and founded the City of Akamantis. Famous now for its abundance of flora and fauna and also the evidence of many Stone Age settlements.

The Avakas Gorge

The Intercontinental Hotel
at Aphodite Hills

Elysium Beach Resort

Pafos Bay

Pafos International Airport (Runway 29 Approach), also the main A6 and coastal roads leading into Pafos Town Centre

Pafos Medieval Castle

Kato Pafos Harbour

Pafos Irrigation Canals

Asprokremmos Dam

The Island's vital water supply flows from the mountains into several huge dams. Asprokremmos Dam collects water from the Xeros Potamos river.

Abandoned Turkish Cypriot Village - Souskiou

Man-made terraces sculpture the mountain environment throughout the North Pafos District

Mavrokolypos Dam

Pafos District - Terraced Farming

The area to the north of Tsada is an amazing mosaic of differing plateaux and the traditional farming ways are evident for as far as the eye can see. Tsada Golf Club is set in the grounds of a 12th Century monastery at 550m. above sea level. It was created by Donald Steel and is a Par 72 - 6208m. course designed in two loops of nine separate holes. The undulating Greens have a superb texture and there are plenty of sand bunkers to trap those misplaced balls

Tsada Golf Club

Tsada Golf Clubhouse

The Tsada fairways are lined with an abundance of mature trees

The Secret Valley Golf Course

Vineyards north of Pissouri - Plantaniskia

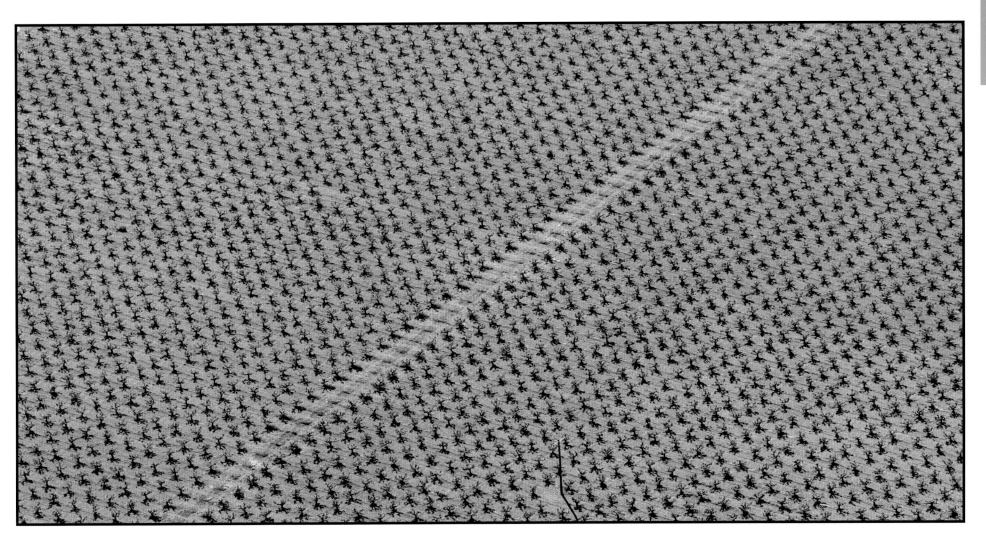

Secret Valley

Pafos Sunbathers

Secret Valley Rock Formations

Secret Valley Clubhouse

Mineral excavation is seen throughout the mountain regions

An Open Air Theatre can often be found in quite small villages

The Pegeia area is famous for having many sea caves and rock formations

The warm clear Mediterranean Sea defines the differing rock layers, through constant erosion

Asprokremmos Dam

The main A6 highway from Limassol to Pafos cuts a winding path through the hillside and across deep ravines

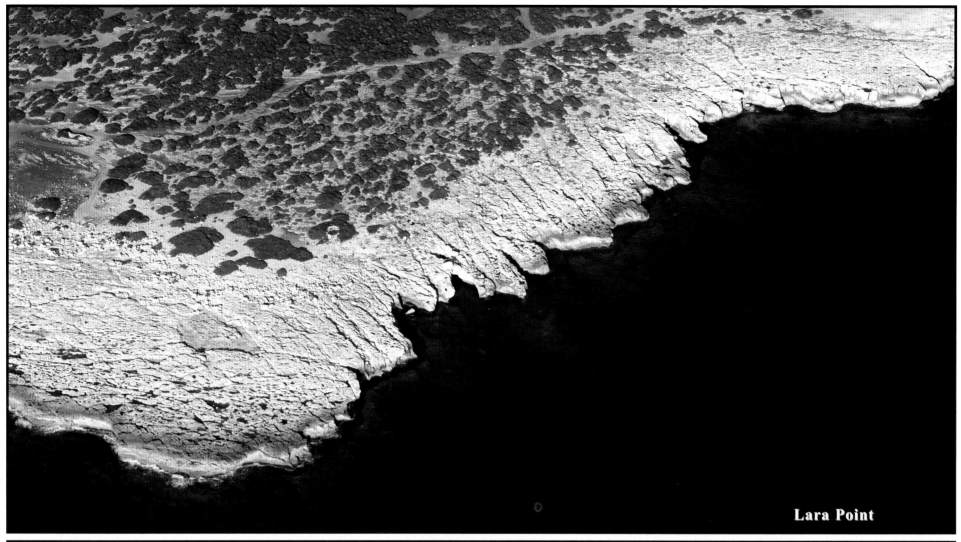

Lara Point

Geronisos Island

Cape Aspro looking towards Petra Tou Romiou and Pafos International Airport. Cape Aspro is a well known nautical landmark

Aphrodite Hills has a championship 18 hole golf course with driving range and a three hole practice course (seen bottom left). The course's signature hole (the seventh) spans the ravine that divides the east and west side of the development

View looking west from overhead Pissouri

Arminou Dam

Tilliria

Aphrodite Hills Golf Villas

The Seventh at Aphrodite Hills Championship Course

Palaipafos - The Sanctuary of Aphrodite at Kouklia

Kynousa

Kart racing in the Chrysochou Bay area

The Pafos Forest

Fire Observation Post

This view towards Pissouri shows the Island's deepest spanned bridge

The typical Pafos Smallholding

Irrigation canals from Asprokremmos Dam

Bay Apartments

Aphodite Hills Clubhouse

Pissouri

Pegeia Sea Caves (Kantarkastoi):
About one hundred million years ago this land was being formed on the ocean floor. The bones and shells of zillions of dead sea creatures piled on top of one another, the sea level then changed as tectonic plates collided and pushed up. This added silt and sand which created the chalky layer seen here. Sea erosion then created the labyrinth of caves, where until recently, seals have been seen

Looking towards Evretou Dam

Episkopi Village

The almost dry Xeros Potamos river feeding the Asprokremmos Dam

Episkopi Village

Evretou Dam

Coral Bay

Pegeia

Pafian Sun Holiday Village

Pegeia

Poseidon Avenue - Pafos

The Anassa (Queen in modern Greek) Beach Hotel

Pafos Amathus Beach Hotel

The Alexander the Great Beach Hotel

The Azia Beach Hotel

The Queens Bay Hotel

The Cynthiana Beach Hotel

The Imperial Beach Hotel

The Annabelle Hotel

Pafos Bay

The Thalassa Hotel

The Elysium Beach Hotel

The Anassa Beach Hotel

Tsada Golf Club

Pegeia

Geronisos Isle

Pegeia

Ostrich Farm.

Polis

St.George Hotel - Pafos

The village of Neo Chorio

Kato Pafos

Limassol and Nicosia Area

After our initial climb-out towards the east, we pass Cape Aspro and then we find Pissouri Bay with the impressive new Columbia Beach Resort Hotel. This luxury Hotel has an impressive pool and offers sport and leisure facilities including two top quality glass-backed Squash courts. The picturesque Village of Pissouri is situated on the high ground overlooking the Bay and is now undergoing considerable development, not withstanding which, the typical Cypriot character has been preserved throughout. Pissouri is famous for numerous vineyards and fine tavernas.

Continuing east towards Limassol we pass the Sovereign Bay Area which is under British Military Control, and cannot be recorded here for security reasons. However, we can show some parts of it such as Avdimou Bay, Kourion Beach, the restored Amphitheatre, and the ruins. Archaeological evidence and historical sources attest to the fact that Kourion was one of the most important Kingdoms of ancient Cyprus. Kourion is built on the imposing heights that dominate the area and would have controlled the fertile river valley (today called Kouris). Excavations here have uncovered much evidence linked to the Hellensic and Roman years, which contribute to the Kourion of the Cypro-Classical Era. Also to be found at the site, are relics of the Cypro-Archaic period 500-475 BC. Following the river Kouris, takes us north to the vast Dam of the same name and the village of Alassa.

Moving south again we approach the outskirts of Limassol town and find Kolossi Castle, a fine example of military architecture originally constructed in the thirteenth Century and subsequently rebuilt in today's form in the mid-fifteenth Century.

As we fly east through the much-cultivated land of Asomatos to the north of Akrotiri, we pass the new Limassol Water Park (Fasouri) and start our tour of the Island's largest port. Limassol Port serves most of the Island's seaborne cargo and passenger traffic. It handles two thirds of the total container traffic as well as the entire volume of grain imports.

The coastal town of Limassol, (Lemesos), is also known as the second City and is the Island's largest seaside resort. It is positioned between the ancient towns of Kurium and Amathus. The lively character of its people matches the Town's carefree holiday atmosphere and long Promenade. The eastern side of the town bustles with night-life and some of the Island's best-known festivals are staged here. Close to the sea, we find all types of hotel accommodation, also luxury apartments and villas. Nearby, there is a wide range of tavernas, pubs, discos and nightclubs. Along the twenty kilometre seafront from Lady's Mile Beach to the Amathus area there are more fine beaches and water-sport facilities. One can also tour the wineries and taste the local produce. Near to the Old Port stands Limassol Castle, built in the fourteenth Century on the site of an earlier Byzantine castle. It was here that Richard the Lionheart allegedly married Queen Berengaria of Navarre in 1191 and crowned her Queen of England, the first Coronation to take place outside England.

The Amathus area, near Agios Tychonas, was one of the largest ancient kingdoms on the Island; it was a Royal City according to legend and historical evidence. It was heavily populated at least three thousand years ago and the name comes from Amathusa, the mother of King Kinyras from Pafos. Until 1191, when Richard the Lionheart arrived in Cyprus, Amathus had been in decline. The tombs had been plundered and much of the stone edifices were taken to Limassol for new construction purposes. More recently, a great many stones were again removed and used in the construction of the Suez Canal. There are now plans to restore the old Amathus fishing Harbour, which is still visible just below the surface of the sea.

After our tour of Governors Beach (Kalymnos), Kalavasos Dam and Germasogeia Dam, we head north over Platres, Prodromi and Troodos, before entering the Nicosia District.

The City of Nicosia (Lefkosia) is the only militarily divided Capital City in the World today. The inner circle of the Old City is defined by a Venetian Wall with eleven Bastions. Roughly half of the inner City remains under Turkish military occupation and the Turkish flag is defiantly displayed on the foothills of the Pentadaktylos Mountain Range.

Limassol Port

Sfalangiotisa Monastery

Nicosia has a rich history that dates back to the Bronze Age. It became the Island's capital in the 11th Century AD. The Lusignans expanded the city with over fifty churches and a magnificent Royal Palace. Today the bustling city blends perfectly with it's historic past, the expansion outside the inner city walls is clearly seen from high above and it now has five municipalities. The new Nicosia has become a contemporary, cosmopolitan business and cultural centre.

Free walking tours organised by the Cyprus Tourism Organisation give an exceptional chance for the visitor to get acquainted with the character of the Old City.

Starting Point: C.T.O. Office (Laiki Geitonia) on Mondays and Thursdays at 10:00 Tel: 22 67 42 64

Moving south to a point 40 km north of Larnaka, perched high on a mountain peak, we find the impressive Stavrovouni Monastery. It was founded in the 14th century by Saint Helena, mother of Constantine the Great, who left a fragment of the Holy Cross to the monastery. The brotherhood is extremely devout, keeping vows as strict as the Mount Athos brotherhood in Greece. Men may visit this monastery from sunrise to sunset however women are not allowed inside. On a clear day the views all around are quite stunning.

Stavrovouni looking North

Stavrovouni looking West

Larnaka

Larnaka is a Town with strong links to the past, in its centre one finds the remains of the ancient city-kingdom of Kition. The Mycenaean Greeks fortified the town with cyclopean walls in the 12th Century and the Phoenicians founded a powerful kingdom here in the 9th Century. Kition was the birthplace of the philosopher Zeno, founder of the Stoic School. In the 18th century it became a centre of commerce and the seat of the European consulate.

The palm tree lined Promenade: the fort and old quarters, give Larnaka its unique character. The nearby lake, is an annual stop-off point for thousands of migrating birds, such as the Flamingo.

Larnaka is also World famous for the Zenobia, a ferry which sank half a mile out from the port. Experts proclaim this to be one of the best wreck diving sites in the world. To this day no one knows the true reason for its loss but the reports said that it encountered technical problems and could not be towed back to port; stating that it would effectively have sealed-off the port entrance. There are other more sinister rumours but what is clear is that nothing creates more of a diving adventure than one that hides a secret.

The ghostly shape of the Zenobia, just twelve metres below the surface

Cape Aspro - Columbia Bay

Columbia Beach Resort Complex

Kouris Dam

Platres

Columbia Beach Resort Hotel

Pissouri

Mediterranean Beach and
Four Seasons Hotels at
Agios Tychonas

Archbishop Makarios III Avenue and St. Nicholas Roundabout - Limassol

Car Imports at Limassol Docks

Atlantica Bay Hotel

Galatex Area

Limassol

Dasoudi Beach Pool

Troodos at 1952 metres above mean sea level is in the clouds and soon to bring precious water to these valleys

Being an Island, Cyprus has a constant flow of container traffic, bringing essential goods from all parts of the Globe

We are living here.

Paramali to Avdimou Bay

Alassa Hills

The Hawaii Grand and
The Elias Beach Hotels

Sanctuary of Apollon Ylatis

Kourion

Kolossi Castle

Amathus Beach Hotel

Limassol Agios Tychonas

Governor's Beach

Le Meridien

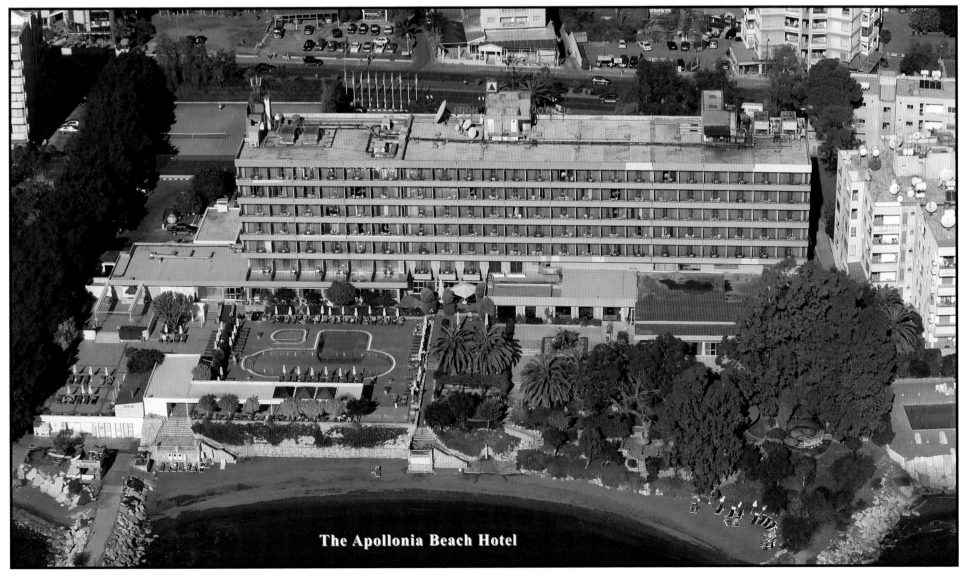

The Apollonia Beach Hotel

Alassa

Asomatos

Dasoudi Bar

Limassol Old Port

Germasogeia Valley

Germasogeia Dam

Pissouri

Tsirion Stadium Limassol

Limassol

The new Limassol Waterpark (Fasouri)

The old Limassol Waterpark

The Polemidia Dam

St Raphael Marina

Paramali Tunnel - A6

Kykkos Monastery

Agios Georgios Alamanos Monastery

Alassa and Kouris Dam

Lefkara Dam

Town Hall Limassol

Limassol Castle

Boat Yard Limassol

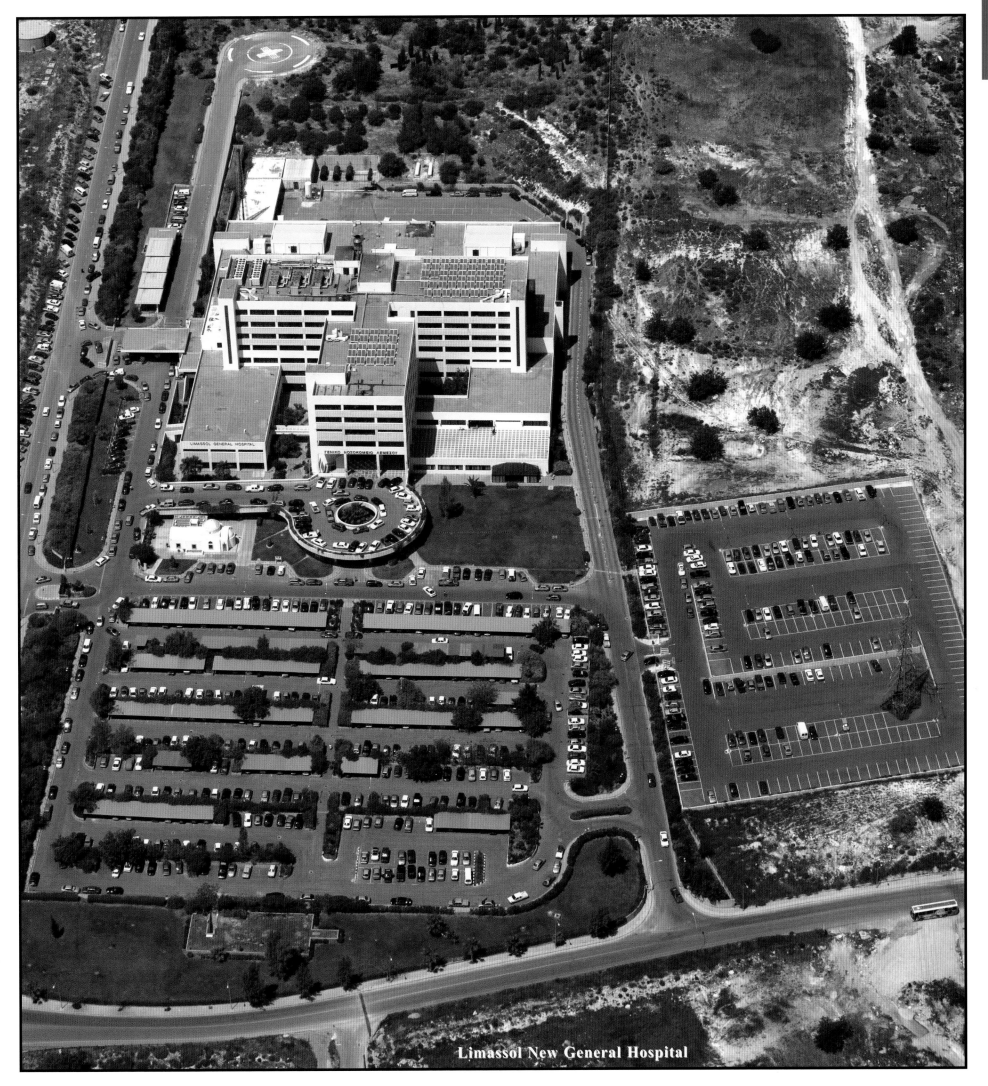

Limassol New General Hospital

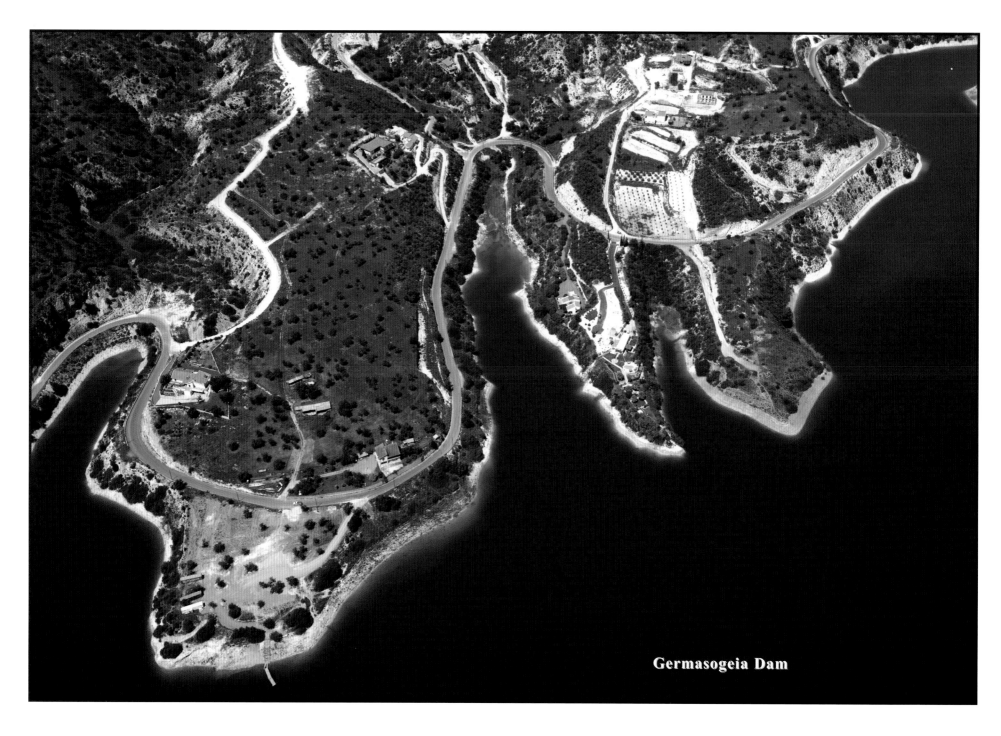

Germasogeia Dam

Agios Sozomenos

Lady's Mile Beach

Bee Hives

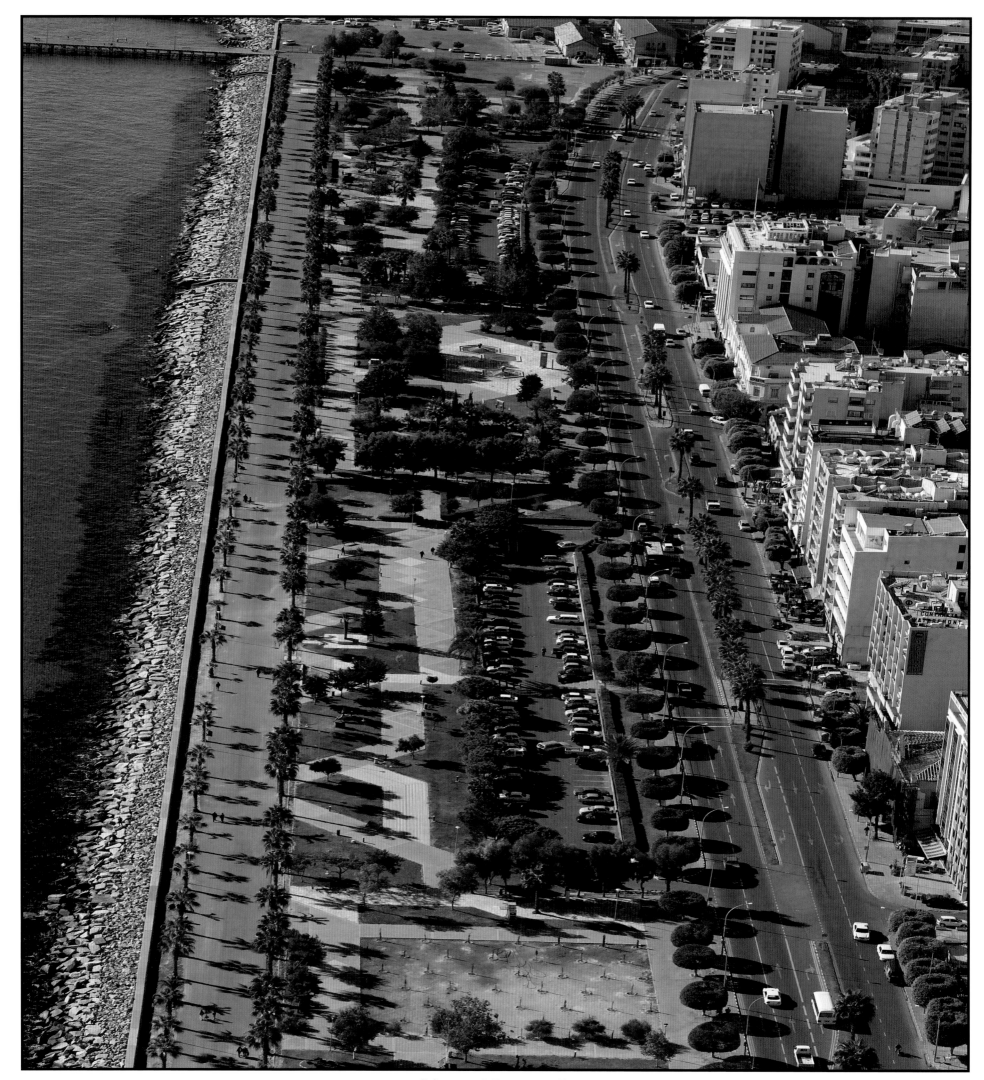

Limassol Promenade

Kalavasos Tenta Neolithic Site 700-600 BC

Agios Tychonas - The Amathous Old Harbour remains can be seen botton right

Nicosia
(Lefkosia)

Kotsiatis

GSP Stadium Nicosia

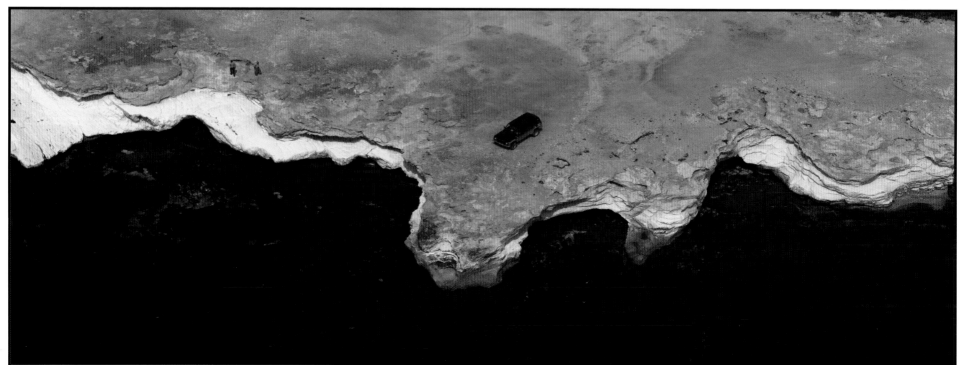

Panayia Tsampika

Stavrovouni Monastery

Kochi

The 18th Century Aquaduct - Kamares

Pedhoulas

Prodromos

Stavrovouni to Larnaka

Stock Exchange Roundabout - Nicosia

GSP Stadium Nicosia

Laiki - The Cyprus Popular Bank HQ

End of season skiing at Mount Olympus

Lympia

The Tomb of Archbishop Makarios III

Xylofagou - Kokkinochoria

Larnaka Marina

Klavdhia

The Breathtaking Terrain - A Brief Geological Explanation

Throughout these pages one cannot fail to see the uniqueness of the Cyprus landscape. The formation of Cyprus was the result of a series of complicated geological events, which have made the Island a geological showcase. Around ninety to one hundred million years ago when still on the bottom of the seabed, tectonic movements resulted in the collision of the African and the Eurasian plates. These plates which form the Earth's crust, move around at about the speed that one's fingernails grow and are about fifty miles thick. The resultant collision that took place, forced the ocean bed to rise and give birth to the Island.

The Troodos and Pentadactylos mountain ranges first appeared about twenty million years ago as two islands. The tip of Mount Troodos is in fact a relic of the ocean floor as it was ninety million years ago. Between one and two million years ago the Mesaoria plain appeared between the two islands, the highly tectonised and fractured conditions of the Troodos mass, a consequence of its uplift, caused deep weathering to create a smooth, mature, topographical mantle with a thick covering of diverse soils. These soils combined with microclimates to produce the forests. The weathering of the sedimentary rocks on the foothills gave rise to alkaline and calcium rich soils which today are where the vineyards, carob and olive groves flourish.

It is the mineral wealth of Cyprus that has shaped the historical background more than any other geological phenomenon. Its copper resources were known the World over. Asbestos, Chromate, Ochre, Siena and Terra Verde were also mined and long galleries penetrate several kilometres into the mountainsides. On the periphery of the mountain ranges, copper mines were prolific.

The Island's once extensive forests were consumed intensively in the smelting process for the extraction of copper, ceramics and in the shipbuilding of fleets for conquering raiders. The everyday energy needs of the past took their toll on the Island's forests. It has been estimated that the copper extraction alone would have used 16 times the standing crop that existed at that time. This means that lumbered forestry areas were regenerated many times over to supply this need alone.

The impressive topography has created a favourable climate that produces precipitation in the mountains, feeding the dams and providing the Island with vital resources. In the cooler regions of Troodos, where the rainfall is higher, cherries and plums can be grown almost within sight of the banana plantations on the coast. The higher reaches of the Troodos Range are snow covered for several months of the year, which allows skiing on Mount Olympus, then, less that an hours drive away one can take a swim in the sea.

The Atlantis Theory

As one ponders the pages of this book, it is easy to see that this Island has changed dramatically over a comparatively short timescale. A few thousand years is but a blink of the eye, in terms of Man's evolutionary progress on planet Earth. Two thousand years ago Plato was writing about the legendary Atlantis in his works Timaeus and Critia and referred to manuscripts that have long since disappeared. Science and explorations however, have revealed that the mythology and legend of that lost civilisation may have been based on a people that dwelt on a land-mass in the north east corner of the Mediterranean, the remains of which are still above water, and are today called Cyprus.

Tennis at Dhekelia Garrison and Officer's Club

The Aldiana Hotel Hobie Cats

Vasilikos Dam

The Aldiana Hotel

Pleasure boats at Limanaki - Agia Napa

Kotsiatis

The South-East to Protaras

As we leave the Larnaka area and head east around the Bay, we pass overhead Dhekelia, this is the central area of the British Sovereign Base which has operated here since the days of the Cold War. The first thing that catches the eye as we progress deeper into the Eastern corner of the Island is how the colour of the soil has changed to a rustic shade of red. In Greek, Kokkinochoria means "fields with red soil" it is the metallic oxides common to this area that cause this phenomenon. The Kokkinochoria area is defined as the land forming a triangle between Famagusta, Cape Greco and Larnaka Bay and is predominantly an agricultural area. The traditional Cyprus potato is grown here.

Protaras has built up a deserving reputation for its windmills and glorious beaches. The crystal clear sea that is common all around this area makes it a water-sports paradise. The Agia Napa night life is famous the world over, and is of course more suited for the younger generation. During the day there is just about everything one could possibly want from bungee jumping to water-skiing or parascending. At night the clubbing just goes on and on until the sun comes up again.

The charming scenery around Agia Napa includes a small fishing harbour which also operates pleasure trips. A monastery dedicated to 'Our Lady of the Forests' stands in the middle of the village and is surrounded by a high wall. It's 16th Century church is partly under ground and cuts into the rock. The hostel to the west of the church, belongs to the World Council of Churches and has a sycamore tree planted by the south gate that is said to be more than 600 years old. A Marine Life Museum is situated within the premises of the Agia Napa Municipality.

As we come to the end of our journey, I can see that we have logged something in the order of 25 flying hours, and taken more than 2000 pictures of Cyprus. We have only 192 pages to fill so not everything can find a place this time around. Our task is nevertheless a long way from complete and I expect that we will continue to document this Island for many years to come. The essence of aerial photography is found in the art of seeing what is there and my feelings are that I have still some way to go before this task reaches its final rendition.

Denny Rowland 2005

Kokkinochoria - The Red Soil Villages

Protaras

Adams Beach Hotel

The Aeneas Hotel

Konnos Bay

Waterworld Water Park at Agia Napa

Agia Napa Sea Caves

The Olympic Lagoon Resort

Waterworld Water Park - the Island's largest

Makronissos - The Dome and Asterias Beach Hotels

Romantzo - Ormideia

Zenon Stadium Larnaka

Cape Pyla Fishing Harbour

Sterna Point

Fig Tree Bay

Grecian Park Hotel at the National Park, Konnos Bay

**Sandy Bay - awarded the blue flag by Agia Napa Municipality -
Pavlo Napa, Anonymous and Tasia Maris Beach Hotels**

Nissi Bay Agia Napa

Nissi Beach

Agia Napa Fishing Harbour - Limanaki

The Aeneas Hotel

Nissi Watersports

Makronissos Beach

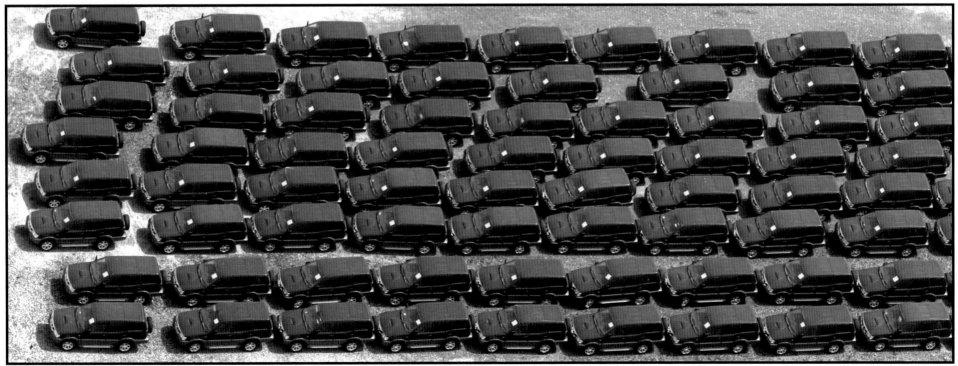

Agia Napa

Agia Napa Nissi Beach

Agia Napa Fishing Harbour

Cape Greco (Gkreko)

Protaras

Fishing Boats at Dhekelia

THE END